# KIM ANDERSON
# ENDLESS DREAMS

# KIM ANDERSON
# ENDLESS DREAMS

teNeues    ARTMERCHANDISING
           & MEDIA AG

FOR ALL CHILDREN AROUND THE WORLD AND FOR EVERYONE WHO IS YOUNG AT HEART.

FÜR DIE KLEINEN UND GROSSEN KINDER DIESER WELT.

# CONTENTS
## INHALT

# CONTENTS

# INHALT

# CONTENTS
## INHALT

## INTRODUCTION

THE NAME KIM ANDERSON IS SYNONYMOUS THROUGHOUT THE WORLD WITH PHOTOGRAPHS OF CHILDREN THAT LOVINGLY REFLECT THE WORLD OF ADULTS. THESE DELICATE IMAGES LEAD THE VIEWER BACK INTO HIS OR HER OWN PAST AND CONJURE UP THE WONDERFUL MOMENTS OF BECOMING A GROWN-UP. THE CHILDREN'S DELICATE FACES, LARGE EYES AND NATURAL DEMEANORS CAPTURE OUR ATTENTION, STIMULATE OUR IMAGINATION AND LET US ONCE AGAIN TAKE PART IN THOSE UNFORGETTABLE MOMENTS OF CHILDHOOD. THROUGH THESE PHOTOGRAPHS, WE DISCOVER THE JOY AND TENDERNESS THAT CAN ONLY BE CONVEYED BY CHILDREN.

INSPIRED BY HIS OWN TWO CHILDREN TO VIEW THE WORLD AS ONLY A CHILD CAN, BERTRAM BAHNER, UNDER THE PSEUDONYM KIM ANDERSON, CREATED THESE WONDERFUL PICTURES.

BERTRAM BAHNER'S INSPIRATION TO CREATE SUCH IMAGES FIRST CAME TO HIM IN 1989 WHILE PHOTOGRAPHING HIS THREE-YEAR-OLD DAUGHTER AND HER FRIEND. AS PART OF AN ANNIVERSARY CELEBRATION IN BONN, WHERE BERTRAM BAHNER LIVED AT THE TIME, SEVERAL STEAM ENGINES AND HISTORIC TRAINS WERE ON DISPLAY AT THE TRAIN STATION. REALIZING THAT THE EXHIBITION CREATED AN UNIQUE ATMOSPHERE FOR PHOTOGRAPHY, BERTRAM BAHNER DECIDED TO TAKE THE GROUP OF CHILDREN THERE TO BE PHOTOGRAPHED. THE CHILDREN WERE SUPPOSED TO DRESS IN KEEPING WITH THE OCCASION, BUT SINCE THEY DIDN'T HAVE THE APPROPRIATE CLOTHES THEY WORE ADULT ATTIRE. THEIR APPEARANCE RAISED A SMILE. THE SWEATERS LOOKED LIKE LONG KNITTED JACKETS, THE LEISURE JACKETS LIKE TRENCH COATS. NEEDLESS TO SAY, THE OVERSIZED HATS ADDED THEIR OWN VERY SPECIAL ALLURE. CLAD IN SUCH GARB, THE LITTLE GROUP ARRIVED IN THE EARLY MORNING AT THE STATION BEFORE THE PLATFORM FILLED UP WITH VISITORS.

WITH THE EXHIBITION AS A BACKDROP, BERTRAM BAHNER LET THE CHILDREN PLAY AS THEY WANTED – THIS EXCEEDED ALL HIS CREATIVE EXPECTATIONS. THE WAY THE CHILDREN INTERACTED – CARRYING THEIR BAGS TO THE TRAIN, WAIVING WITH A LAUGH FROM THE RAILROAD CAR AND HUGGING ONE ANOTHER – TOLD AN UNIQUE STORY.

ON THIS DAY MEMORIES WERE CAPTURED IN PHOTOGRAPHS THAT TODAY ARE AMONG THE CLASSICS OF THE KIM ANDERSON COLLECTION. AT THE SAME TIME, THE "FAMILY OUTING" MADE THEM EAGER TO PURSUE NEW EXPERIENCES.

TODAY, BERTRAM BAHNER WATCHES THE "LITTLE ADULTS" WITH A GREAT DEAL OF PATIENCE, OBSERVING HOW THEY UNAFFECTEDLY TRY TO IMITATE THEIR SURROUNDINGS. AFTER MANY YEARS, HIS PHOTOGRAPHY HAS RESULTED IN HIS BEING ABLE TO EMPATHIZE WITH HIS CHILDREN.

THE KIM ANDERSON COLLECTION IS COMPRISED OF SOME 800 ORIGINAL, HAND-COLORED MOTIFS FROM ALL AREAS OF LIFE. THIS BOOK CONTAINS A SELECTION OF RECENT, FORMERLY UNPUBLISHED PHOTOGRAPHS, ALL EXECUTED IN LOCATIONS NEAR THE ARTIST'S HOME.

DER NAME KIM ANDERSON STEHT WELTWEIT FÜR KINDERFOTOGRAFIE, DIE AUF EINE LIEBEVOLLE ART DIE WELT DER ERWACHSENEN REFLEKTIERT. DIESE EINFÜHLSAMEN AUFNAHMEN FÜHREN DEN BETRACHTER ZURÜCK IN DIE EIGENE VERGANGENHEIT UND ERINNERN AN DIE WUNDERVOLLEN MOMENTE DES ERWACHSENWERDENS. ES SIND VOR ALLEM DIE ZARTEN KINDERGESICHTER MIT IHREN GROSSEN AUGEN, DIE MIT IHRER NATÜRLICHKEIT DEN BLICK DES BETRACHTERS ANZIEHEN, ERINNERUNGEN WECKEN, UNSERE FANTASIE ANREGEN UND UNS AN ALL DIESEN UNVERGESSLICHEN AUGENBLICKEN TEILHABEN LASSEN. WIR ENTDECKEN MOMENTE DER ZÄRTLICHKEIT UND DER FREUDE, WIE SIE UNS NUR KINDER NAHE BRINGEN KÖNNEN.

BERTRAM BAHNER IST DER KÜNSTLER, WELCHER UNTER DEM PSEUDONYM KIM ANDERSON DIESE WUNDERBAREN BILDER GESCHAFFEN HAT. ER IST SELBST VATER ZWEIER KINDER, DIE IHN INSPIRIERT HABEN, SICH AUF DIE EBENE DER KINDER ZU BEGEBEN UND DIE WELT EINMAL AUS DEREN SICHT ZU BETRACHTEN.

SEINE BEGEISTERUNG FÜR DIE KINDERFOTOGRAFIE BEGANN 1989, ALS ER DIE ERSTEN BILDER VON SEINER DAMALS 3 1/2-JÄHRIGEN TOCHTER UND IHREM SPIELKAMERADEN AUFNAHM. ANLÄSSLICH EINER JUBILÄUMSFEIER IN SEINEM DAMALIGEN WOHNORT BONN WAREN AUF

DEM BAHNHOF DAMPFLOKOMOTIVEN UND HISTORISCHE ZÜGE ANGEKÜNDIGT. UM DIESE EINMALIGE STIMMUNG ZU NUTZEN, VERABREDETE SICH DIE KLEINE GRUPPE DORT AM NÄCHSTEN TAG. DA DIE KINDER DEM ANLASS ENTSPRECHEND ANGEZOGEN SEIN SOLLTEN, PASSENDE KLEIDUNGSSTÜCKE ABER NICHT GRIFFBEREIT WAREN, ZWECKENTFREMDETE MAN KURZERHAND DIE KLEIDUNG DER ERWACHSENEN. DER ANBLICK WAR ZUM SCHMUNZELN, DENN AN DEN KINDERN SAH EIN PULLOVER AUS WIE EIN STRICKMANTEL UND EINE FREIZEITJACKE WIE EIN TRENCHCOAT. DIE ÜBERGROSSEN HÜTE HATTEN SOWIESO IHREN GANZ BESONDEREN REIZ. SO AUSGESTATTET WAR DAS KLEINE FOTOTEAM DANN AM FRÜHEN MORGEN AM BAHNHOF, NOCH BEVOR SICH DIE BAHNSTEIGE MIT BESUCHERN FÜLLTEN.

VOR DIESER KULISSE ÜBERLIESS BERTRAM BAHNER DIE KINDER IHRER SPIELERISCHEN WELT, WELCHE ALS KREATIVE QUELLE ALLE ERWARTUNGEN ÜBERTRAF. ALLEINE DIE ART, WIE SIE MITEINANDER UMGINGEN, DEN KOFFER ZUM ZUG SCHLEPPTEN, LACHEND AUS DEM EISENBAHNWAGON WINKTEN UND SICH UMARMTEN, ERZÄHLT EINE UNNACHAHMLICHE BILDERGESCHICHTE.

AN DIESEM TAG ENTSTANDEN EINERSEITS FOTOGRAFISCHE ERINNERUNGEN, WELCHE HEUTE ZU DEN KLASSIKERN DER KIM ANDERSON COLLECTION ZÄH-

LEN, ANDERERSEITS MACHTE DIESER „FAMILIENAUSFLUG" NEUGIERIG AUF WEITERE ERLEBNISSE.

AUCH HEUTE NOCH BEOBACHTET BERTRAM BAHNER MIT VIEL GEDULD DIE „KLEINEN ERWACHSENEN", WIE SIE AUF EINE UNGEZWUNGENE ART UND WEISE VERSUCHEN, DAS ZU IMITIEREN, WAS SIE IN IHRER UMGEBUNG WAHRNEHMEN. SO HAT ER SICH AUCH VIELE JAHRE NACH SEINEN ERSTEN AUFNAHMEN SEIN EINFÜHLUNGSVERMÖGEN FÜR DIE WELT DER KINDER BEWAHRT.

DIE KIM ANDERSON COLLECTION UMFASST HEUTE ETWA 800 ORIGINAL HANDKOLORIERTE FOTOGRAFIEN AUS ALLEN LEBENSBEREICHEN. DIESES BUCH IST EINE AUSWAHL NEUESTER UNVERÖFFENTLICHTER AUFNAHMEN, WELCHE ALLE AN AUSGEWÄHLTEN PLÄTZEN IN DER NÄHE DES WOHNORTES DES KÜNSTLERS ENTSTANDEN SIND.

YOU LOOKED STUNNING IN YOUR RED COAT ...

I HARDLY DARED TO SPEAK TO YOU ...

WUNDERSCHÖN SAHST DU AUS IN DEM ROTEN MANTEL ...

ICH TRAUTE MICH KAUM DICH ANZUSPRECHEN ...

... THEN YOU LOOKED OVER AT ME – AND I WAS ENCHANTED!

... DANN HAST DU ZU MIR HERÜBERGESCHAUT – UND ICH WAR VERZAUBERT!

... YOU WERE AMAZED BY THE LOUD, ROARING SOUND OUTSIDE YOUR FRONT DOOR.
I WANTED TO SURPRISE YOU ...
... WIE HAST DU GESTAUNT, ÜBER DAS LAUT KNATTERNDE GERÄUSCH VOR DEINER
HAUSTÜR. ICH WOLLTE DICH ÜBERRASCHEN ...

… YOU GOT YOUR CAMERA AT ONCE. I WAS YOUR ABSOLUTE STAR!

… DU HAST SOFORT DIE KAMERA GEHOLT. ICH WAR DEIN ABSOLUTER STAR!

I SERVED, AND YOU RETURNED THE BALL WELL. YOU WON THAT RALLY, AND I MADE THE "BIG POINTS". BUT YOU ARE THE WINNER OF THE GAME THAT REALLY COUNTS – YOU´RE THE CHAMPION OF MY LIFE!

ICH HATTE AUFSCHLAG, DU HAST SOUVERÄN GEKONTERT. KLEINE BALLWECHSEL HAST DU GEWONNEN, ICH MACHTE DIE „BIG POINTS". ABER DAS ENTSCHEIDENDE SPIEL GEHT AN DICH – DU BIST DER CHAMP MEINES LEBENS!

OF LIFE

23

I SPENT COUNTLESS HOURS

TRYING TO IMPRESS YOU ...

UNZÄHLIGE STUNDEN HABE ICH

INVESTIERT, UM DIR ZU IMPONIEREN ...

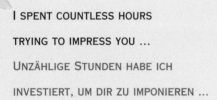

You just laughed at me and drove with me to the ends of the earth ...

Du hast mich einfach angelacht und bist mit mir ans Ende der Welt gefahren ...

THE $HOPPING SPREE WAS A
SMASHING SUCCESS!
DIE $HOPPING-TOUR WAR EIN
VOLLER ERFOLG!

IN THE CAFE AFTERWARDS, THE DESSERT MENU
WINKED AT US. BIG PIECES OF CAKE WERE HIDDEN
UNDER SMALL PORTIONS OF WHIPPED CREAM …

IM CAFÉ LACHTE UNS DANACH DIE DESSERTKARTE AN. GANZE
TORTENSTÜCKE VERSTECKTEN SICH UNTER EINER KLEINEN PORTION SAHNE …

... AND THERE WERE LARGE SCOOPS OF

ICE CREAM, TOO ... WE FOUND THEM ALL!

... AUCH GROSSE EISKUGELN DRÄNGTEN SICH DARUNTER

... WIR HABEN SIE ALLE GEFUNDEN!

WE DIDN´T REALLY WANT TO LEAVE
HOME AT ALL.

EIGENTLICH WOLLTEN WIR GAR NICHT
VON ZU HAUSE WEG.

BUT WE WEREN'T BORED FOR A SECOND!

OUR VACATION AT THE FARM WENT BY

LIKE LIGHTNING.

ABER KEINE SPUR VON LANGEWEILE!

DIE FERIEN AUF DEM BAUERNHOF

VERGINGEN WIE IM FLUG.

We made all kinds of plans, acted silly, were inseparable.

Zusammen schmiedeten wir allerlei Pläne, machten Blödsinn und waren unzertrennlich.

FRIENDS FOREVER

IT WAS A TIME OF ADVENTURE AND OF PLAYING HIDE-AND-SEEK.

ES WAR DIE ZEIT DER ABENTEUER UND DES VERSTECKSPIELENS.

WHEN WE SAID GOODBYE – DO YOU REMEMBER – WE ALMOST CRIED.

BEIM ABSCHIED – WEISST DU NOCH – HABEN WIR FAST GEWEINT.

How we laughed when you blocked
my way and insisted that I take off
my shoes!
Wie haben wir gelacht, als du
mir den Weg versperrtest und
darauf bestanden hast, dass
ich die Schuhe ausziehe!

... suddenly you grabbed the
broom and swept the whole barn.
... Auf einmal hast du dir einfach
den Besen geschnappt und die
ganze Scheune gefegt.

IT'S TRUE ... FOR SOMETHING SWEET I'D STOP WHATEVER I WAS DOING AND
FORGET THE WORLD AROUND ME. TIME STOPPED – AND I WOULDN'T HAVE TRADED
THAT MOMENT FOR ANYTHING IN THE WORLD!

ES STIMMT ... FÜR ETWAS SÜSSES KONNTE ICH ALLES LIEGEN LASSEN UND DIE
WELT UM MICH HERUM VERGESSEN. DIE ZEIT HIELT AN – UND GEGEN NICHTS AUF
DER WELT HÄTTE ICH DIESEN MOMENT TAUSCHEN WOLLEN!

A VERY SPECIAL PRESENT WAS
WAITING FOR ME.
EIN GANZ BESONDERES GESCHENK
WARTETE AUF MICH.

SHE WAS SWEET ... I WAS SUPPOSED TO GUESS WHAT IT WAS.

SIE WAR SÜSS ... ICH SOLLTE RATEN WAS ES IST.

# PRESENT

Of course I had an idea — but I went along with it ...

Natürlich hatte ich eine Vorstellung — tat aber völlig ahnungslos ...

I COULDN´T HAVE IMAGINED BEING WITHOUT MY MOUSE …

UNTIL ONE DAY I KISSED IT ON ITS STUB NOSE.

NIEMALS HÄTTE ICH MIR VORSTELLEN KÖNNEN, OHNE MEINE MAUS ZU SEIN …

BIS ICH SIE EINES TAGES AUF IHRE STUPSNASE KÜSSTE.

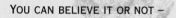

YOU CAN BELIEVE IT OR NOT –

BUT IT SUDDENLY TURNED INTO A LITTLE PRINCE!

OB IHR ES GLAUBT ODER NICHT –

SIE VERWANDELTE SICH PLÖTZLICH IN EINEN KLEINEN PRINZEN!

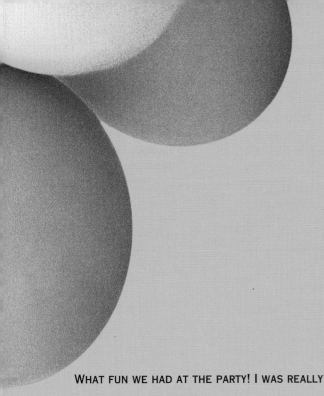

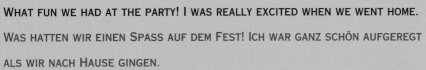

WHAT FUN WE HAD AT THE PARTY! I WAS REALLY EXCITED WHEN WE WENT HOME.

WAS HATTEN WIR EINEN SPASS AUF DEM FEST! ICH WAR GANZ SCHÖN AUFGEREGT

ALS WIR NACH HAUSE GINGEN.

AND THEN WHEN YOU KISSED ME I ALMOST WENT UP WITH THE BALLOONS ...

ALS DU MICH DANN NOCH GEKÜSST HAST, WÄRE ICH FAST MIT DEN

LUFTBALLONS ABGEHOBEN ...

IT WAS EASY AS PIE TO BE IN LOVE.

ES WAR KINDERLEICHT, VERLIEBT

ZU SEIN.

IN COUNTLESS LETTERS WE
PROMISED EACH OTHER ETERNAL LOVE.
IN UNZÄHLIGEN BRIEFEN
VERSPRACHEN WIR UNS EWIGE LIEBE.

THE MEMORIES HAVE FADED ...

DIE ERINNERUNG IST INZWISCHEN VERBLASST ...

... BUT I HAVE KEPT THE LETTERS UNTIL TODAY.

... DIE BRIEFE ABER HABE ICH BIS HEUTE AUFBEWAHRT.

# WOMEN & SHOES

Oh dear, what shoes should I wear today ...?
... The blue ones that go so well with the
striped dress, the gold ones I bought yesterday,
or my favorite shoes with the checkered pattern?
Welche Schuhe ziehe ich heute bloss an ...?
... Die blauen, die so gut zum gestreiften Kleid
passen, die goldenen, welche ich erst gestern
gekauft habe, oder meine Lieblingsschuhe mit dem
karierten Muster?

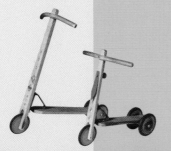

THE BOYS THOUGHT THEY WERE HOT SHOTS. THEY HAD NO IDEA WHY WE WERE LAUGHING SO HARD … DIE JUNGS HIELTEN SICH FÜR DEN MITTELPUNKT DER WELT. SIE HATTEN JA KEINE AHNUNG, WARUM WIR SO LACHTEN …

MY BIG SISTER WAS ALREADY A REAL LADY.

MEINE GROSSE SCHWESTER WAR SCHON EINE RICHTIGE DAME.

She always acted so strangely grown-up …

Sie tat immer so komisch erwachsen …

# MY BIG S

One evening she sat down next to me
and told me everything about her new heartthrob.
Eines Abends hat sie sich zu mir gesetzt
und mir alles von ihrem neuen Schwarm erzählt.

WHEN I GROW UP, I WANT TO BE JUST LIKE HER!

WENN ICH MAL GROSS BIN, MÖCHTE ICH SO SEIN WIE SIE!

I LOOKED EVERYWHERE TO FIND YOU,
YOUR IMAGE ALWAYS IN MY HEART.
ICH HABE ÜBERALL GESUCHT, UM DICH
ZU FINDEN, DAS BILD VON DIR IMMER IN
MEINEM HERZEN.

You accompanied me, were always close by, no matter where I went.

Du hast mich begleitet, warst in meiner Nähe, wohin ich auch ging.

DO YOU RECOGNIZE ME? IT´S ME, YOUR LITTLE SWEETHEART,

WITH A MELODY UNDER MY ARM – JUST FOR YOU!

ERKENNST DU MICH WIEDER? ICH BIN´S, DEIN KLEINER SCHATZ,

MIT EINER MELODIE UNTERM ARM – NUR FÜR DICH!

EVERYTHING WAS SOOO IMPORTANT. AFTER TALKING ON THE PHONE FOR HOURS,

WE MADE A DATE FOR THE AFTERNOON. WE HAD SO MUCH TO TALK ABOUT ...

ALLES WAR SOOO WICHTIG! NACH STUNDENLANGEM TELEFONIEREN VERABREDETEN

WIR UNS FÜR DEN NACHMITTAG. WIR HATTEN UNS SO VIEL ZU ERZÄHLEN ...

# WOMEN TALK

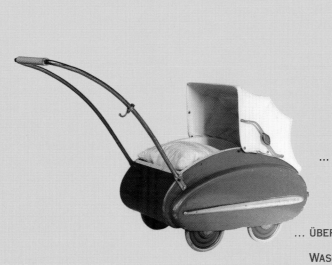

... ABOUT BABY POWDER, HAIRDRESSERS,

PACIFIERS, LAUNDRY DETERGENT,

BANANA BABY FOOD, DIAPERS ...

... ÜBER BABYPUDER, FRISUREN, SCHNULLER,

WASCHMITTEL, BANANENBREI, WINDELN ...

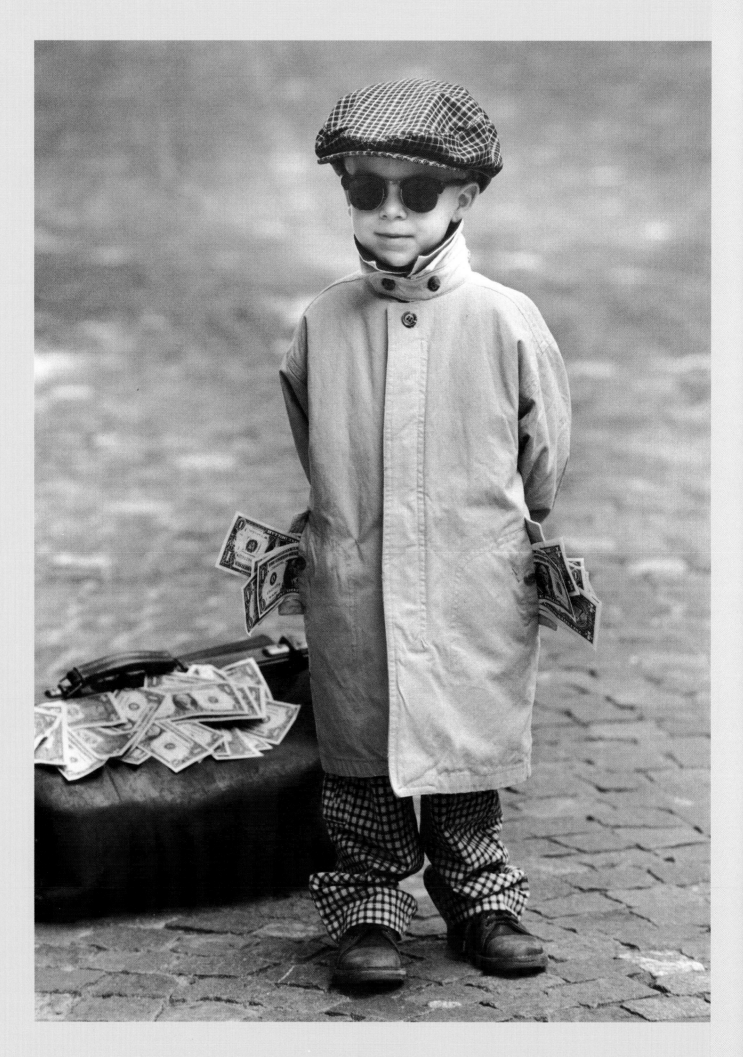

OUR PLAN WAS INGENIOUS!
WEARING DADDY´S SUNGLASSES
NO ONE WOULD RECOGNIZE US.
UNSER PLAN WAR GENIAL!
MIT PAPIS SONNENBRILLEN WÜRDE UNS
NIEMAND ERKENNEN.

# OUR LITTLE GANGSTERS

In the late afternoon we slinked out of the house.
At the next corner, passers-by suddenly spoke to us …
they were our neighbors!
Am späten Nachmittag schlichen wir uns aus dem Haus.
Wir kamen bis zur nächsten Ecke, da sprachen uns plötzlich
Passanten an … es waren unsere Nachbarn!

THEY SAID HELLO, STROKED OUR
HEADS, AND LAUGHED HEARTILY!
SIE GRÜSSTEN UNS, STREICHELTEN
UNS ÜBER DEN KOPF UND LACHTEN
DABEI HERZLICH!

THE OTHER BOYS LIVED A FEW STREETS AWAY. IT WAS SAID THAT THEY HAD
WON EVERY MATCH SO FAR ... BUT WE WEREN´T AFRAID.
DIE ANDEREN JUNGS WOHNTEN EIN PAAR STRASSEN WEITER. ANGEBLICH
HATTEN SIE BISHER JEDES MATCH GEWONNEN ... ABER WIR HATTEN KEINE ANGST.

THE SOCCER GAME

FROM THE LOOK OF US ALONE

WE WERE A STRONG UNIT …

ALLEINE OPTISCH BILDETEN

WIR EINE ÜBERZEUGENDE EINHEIT …

OUR GOALKEEPER´S STRATEGIC TIPS WERE A BLESSING!

DIE STRATEGISCHEN TIPPS UNSERES TORWARTS WAREN GOLD WERT!

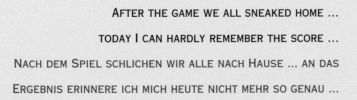

AFTER THE GAME WE ALL SNEAKED HOME ...

TODAY I CAN HARDLY REMEMBER THE SCORE ...

NACH DEM SPIEL SCHLICHEN WIR ALLE NACH HAUSE ... AN DAS

ERGEBNIS ERINNERE ICH MICH HEUTE NICHT MEHR SO GENAU ...

... ADULTS ARE SO VERY WELL ORGANIZED!

WE THOUGHT WE COULD BE, TOO ... SO WE FOUNDED

OUR OWN "CANDY SERVICE."

... DIE ERWACHSENEN SIND JA SO GUT ORGANISIERT!

WIR DACHTEN UNS, DAS KÖNNEN WIR AUCH ... SO HABEN

WIR UNSEREN EIGENEN „BONBON SERVICE" GEGRÜNDET.

# LOVELY DAYS

IT WAS A TIME OF DREAMS AND OF POETRY.

WE CONFIDED OUR EXPERIENCES TO OUR DIARIES.

ES WAR DIE ZEIT DER TRÄUME UND DER POESIE.

UNSERE ERLEBNISSE VERTRAUTEN WIR DEM TAGEBUCH AN.

WE ADORNED THE STORIES WITH ALL THE COLORS OF THE RAINBOW.

DIE GESCHICHTEN SCHMÜCKTEN WIR IN ALLEN REGENBOGENFARBEN AUS.

But we preferred most of all to lie in the

grass and let ourselves be tickled by the sun´s rays.

Am liebsten jedoch lagen wir im Gras

und liessen uns von den Sonnenstrahlen kitzeln.

91

DO YOU REMEMBER? YOU CHOSE THE NAME. I PICKED YOU UP AT THE HOSPITAL.

ERINNERST DU DICH? DU HATTEST DEN NAMEN AUSGESUCHT. ICH HOLTE DICH IM

KRANKENHAUS AB.

I WAS SO PROUD TO PUSH A BABY
CARRIAGE ... FOR EVERYONE TO SEE!
WAS WAR ICH STOLZ, EINEN KINDER-
WAGEN ZU SCHIEBEN ... UND ALLE
KONNTEN ES SEHEN!

WE WERE OVERJOYED AND TOLD EVERYONE.

WIR WAREN ÜBERGLÜCKLICH UND HABEN ES DER GANZEN WELT ERZÄHLT.

O U R   S M

It was one of those sports cars that made your heart beat faster.

Es war einer jener Sportwagen, die das Herz höher schlagen lassen.

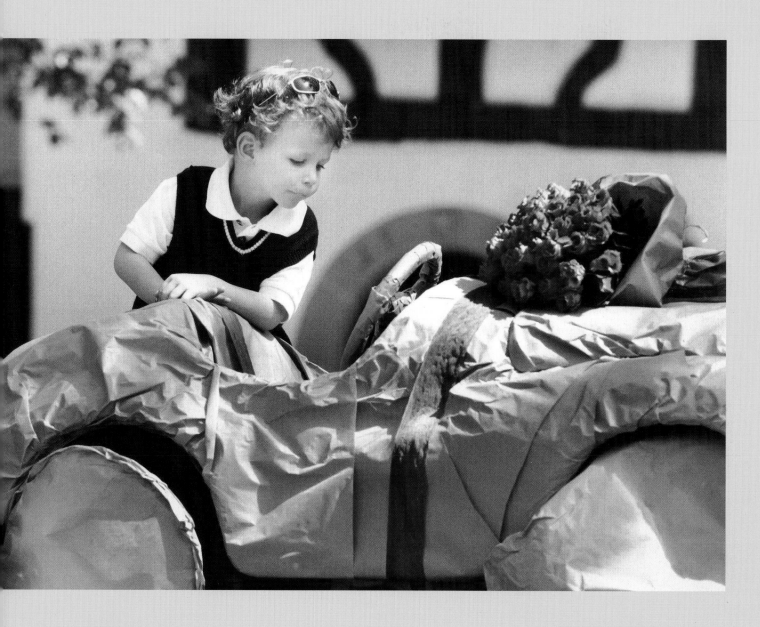

It aroused a feeling of freedom and adventure. One day
I traded it in for a family car ... just for you!

Er weckte das Gefühl von Freiheit und Abenteuer! Eines Tages
tauschte ich ihn gegen ein Familienauto ein ... dir zu liebe!

... DO YOU REMEMBER? YOU COULD HARDLY SLEEP AND
YOU WENT TO THE RAILWAY STATION EARLY THE NEXT MORNING.
... WEISST DU NOCH? DU KONNTEST KAUM SCHLAFEN UND
BIST AN JENEM MORGEN SEHR ZEITIG ZUM BAHNHOF GEGANGEN.

YOU STOOD ON THE PLATFORM AND WAITED FOR ME.

DU HAST AM BAHNSTEIG GESTANDEN UND AUF MICH GEWARTET.

I RUSHED INTO YOUR ARMS AND NEVER LET YOU GO!

ICH BIN IN DEINE ARME GERANNT UND HABE DICH NIE MEHR LOSGELASSEN!

## IMPRESSUM

© 2001 teNeues Verlag GmbH + Co KG, Kempen
KIM ANDERSON® © 2001 NBM Bahner Studios AG, Switzerland
© 2001 ArtMerchandising & Media AG, Munich

Picture and text rights reserved for all countries.
No part of this publication may be reproduced in any manner whatsoever.
All rights reserved.

All photographs and texts by Bertram Bahner
Assistance for photo production by Sandra Hagenbuch
English text edited by Burke Barrett, Cologne
German text edited by Dr. Sabine Werner-Birkenbach, Marbach am Neckar
Production by ArtMerchandising & Media AG, Munich
Design by Merchandising Munich / Creative Team
Project coordination by Sabine Würfel, teNeues Verlag, Kempen
Production by Dieter Haberzettl, teNeues Verlag, Kempen

Licensed by ArtMerchandising & Media AG, www.artmm-ag.com

ArtMerchandising & Media AG
Münchner Strasse 20
D-85774 Unterföhring
Phone: +49 89 / 95 07 86 60, Fax: +49 89 / 95 07 87 60
E-mail: info@artmm-ag.com
www.artmm-ag.com

ArtMedia Group
16 West 22nd Street
New York, NY 10010
Phone: 212 741 4028, Fax: 212 627 9866
E-mail: info@artmediagroup.com
www.artmediagroup.com

Published in the US and Canada by teNeues Publishing Company
Published in Germany by teNeues Verlag GmbH + Co KG
Published in the UK and Ireland by teNeues Publishing UK Ltd.
www.teneues.com

While we strive for utmost precision in every detail, we cannot be held
responsible for any inaccuracies, neither for any subsequent loss or damage
arising.

Die Deutsche Bibliothek – CIP-Einheitsaufnahme

Ein Titeldatensatz für diese Publikation ist bei der Deutschen Bibliothek
erhältlich.

ISBN 3-8238-5490-9
Printed in Italy.